TOP 10 BASKETBALL SUPERSTARS

BY JOHN WALTERS

The Child's World®
childsworld.com

Published by The Child's World®
1980 Lookout Drive • Mankato, MN 56003-1705
800-599-READ • www.childsworld.com

Photo credits:
AP: Tom DiPace 5, 19; Al Messerschmidt 6; Kevork
Djansezian 9; 10; 11; Paul Vathis 12; Reed Saxon 14;
John Swart 18. Dreamstime.com: Chimpinski (cover);
Peter Muzslay 21. Newscom: Stephen Dowell/TNS 7;
Icon Sports Media 8; Torrey Purvery/Icon Sportswire
4, 16; Laura Cavanaugh/UPI 15; Jose Carlos Fajardo/
TNS 17.

ISBN: 9781503827226
LCCN: 2017960456

Printed in the United States of America
PA02380

CONTENTS

Introduction: Who's Number One?. 4

Larry Bird 6

Stephen Curry 7

Tim Duncan 8

"Magic" Johnson 9

Oscar Robertson 10

Bill Russell 11

Wilt Chamberlain 12

Kareem Abdul-Jabbar 14

LeBron James 16

Michael Jordan 18

Your Top Ten! 20

Sports Glossary 22

Find Out More 23

Index/About the Author 24

WHO'S NUMBER ONE?

Who's the greatest basketball player ever? Before you answer, "LeBron James!" you may want to ask your parents or grandparents. Or better yet, look at our list.

Basketball is the ultimate team sport. Everyone must play offense and defense. So choosing the best basketball player is not as simple as seeing who has the most points. LeBron James, for example, has only led the NBA in scoring once in his 15 seasons. Still, almost everyone agrees that he's the greatest player of this century.

How do you rate the best basketball player? Passing matters, too. So does rebounding. And what about winning? How much should you pay attention to that? The player on this Top Ten list with the lowest career scoring average also played on the most championship teams.

LeBron James

Think of it as asking, "Who is the best student in your class?" Is it the kid who is pretty good at every subject? Or is it the kid who wins every spelling bee but is only decent at math? Or is it the one who has perfect attendance but is not the best in any one subject?

Actually, there is no right answer. We just hope you have fun learning about what makes these 10 players the greatest who ever took the court. Then you can go ahead and rank them yourself.

Michael Jordan

NUMBERS, NUMBERS

Sports writer John Hollinger created a way to compare players from different time periods. He called his new stat "Player Efficiency Rating," or PER. Efficiency means doing work at a high level in the least amount of time. The system only goes back to 1973. Still, it's fun to compare players side by side. Here are the top five all-time in PER:

1. Michael Jordan   27.91
2. LeBron James   27.71
3. Shaquille O'Neal   26.43
4. David Robinson   26.18
5. Wilt Chamberlain   26.13

Bird signed with Boston in 1979. He was the highest-paid rookie in sports history at the time.

LARRY BIRD

BOSTON CELTICS

Why did they call him "Larry Legend"? Because when the Celtics needed a game-winning play, Larry Bird always came through.

A 12-time All-Star, Bird checked all the boxes of greatness: Rookie of the Year, NBA MVP (three times), NBA Finals MVP (twice), and All-Star Game MVP. He also led the Celtics to five NBA Finals in his first eight seasons, winning three of them.

The Indiana native was the first NBA player to average better than 50 percent from the field, 40 percent from beyond the **three-point arc**, and 90 percent from the free throw line. That is now known as the 50-40-90 Club, and Bird founded it.

Bird's brilliance is not only measured in stats or trophies. He was simply one of the smartest and most confident players ever to lace up sneakers.

NUMBERS, NUMBERS

Seven players in NBA history have put together 50-40-90 seasons. Only Bird and Steve Nash have done so more than once. Bird had two such seasons and Nash, who retired in 2014, had four.

6

STEPHEN CURRY

GOLDEN STATE WARRIORS

Curry's coach, Steve Kerr, is the NBA's all-time leader in three-point field-goal percentage (45.4).

When he was in college, people wondered if Stephen Curry would be able to survive in the NBA. He was skinny and baby-faced. To some, he looked like a seventh grader. The son of a former NBA player, Curry never doubted himself. Today he is considered the greatest shooter in NBA history.

The NBA introduced the three-point shot in 1979. Before Curry's rookie season in 2009, only three players had ever made 250 threes in a season. Curry has done it *five* times. In the 2015-16 season, he became the first player to top 400 threes in one season. No other NBA player has ever made 300!

Curry is more than accurate; he is a winner. Before he joined Golden State, they had only one NBA title. Since 2014, he has led his team to two NBA championships. In 2015-16, he led them to the best record (73-9) in NBA history.

NUMBERS, NUMBERS
Top Three-Point Seasons Ever
1. Curry, 402 (2015-16)
2. Curry, 324 (2016-17)
3. Curry, 286 (2014-15)
4. Klay Thompson, 276 (2015-16)
5. Curry, 272 (2012-13)

As a senior at Wake Forest, Duncan was named the national player of the year.

TIM DUNCAN

SAN ANTONIO SPURS

The season before the Spurs drafted the 6-11 Tim Duncan, they finished 20-62. The following year, San Antonio finished 56-26. That's the best single-season turnaround ever.

Considered the greatest **power forward** ever to play the game, Duncan was born on St. Croix. That's an island in the Caribbean Sea that is a U.S. territory. As a boy he was an excellent swimmer. Then a hurricane destroyed the island's pools, so he picked up a basketball.

After college at Wake Forest, Duncan led the Spurs to five NBA championships. The Spurs never missed the playoffs and won at least 50 games in all of his 19 full seasons. Duncan did everything right. With his long arms he was an outstanding defender. He was also a 15-time All-Star. There were players who made more highlight reels, but no player since Michael Jordan was more widely respected.

NUMBERS, NUMBERS

Duncan is second all-time in postseason games played.

Derek Fisher	259
Tim Duncan	251
Robert Horry	244

"MAGIC" JOHNSON

LOS ANGELES LAKERS

The NBA does not keep stats on smiles, but Earvin "Magic" Johnson would easily be the all-time leader. Magic led the Los Angeles Lakers to five NBA championships in his first nine seasons. What he did best was make basketball fun.

Johnson played point guard but stood 6-9. Most point guards are much shorter. He became the only player to average more than 11 **assists** per game. Magic's job was to pass the ball to an open teammate and make them look good. His job was to be unselfish. He did this better than anyone and he made the Lakers fun to watch in the 1980s.

He later showed great courage when he got the disease AIDS. He has raised money for research and helped many people who also have AIDS.

NUMBERS, NUMBERS
Helping Out

Magic is the NBA's all-time leader in playoff assists.

Magic Johnson	2,346
John Stockton	1,839
LeBron James	1,489

In Game 6 of the 1980 NBA Finals, Magic stepped in to play center and lead L.A. to victory.

OSCAR ROBERTSON

CINCINNATI ROYALS • MILWAUKEE BUCKS

"The Big O" filled up the stats sheet. In 1962, he became the first NBA player to average a **triple-double** for an entire season. Only one player, Russell Westbrook of Oklahoma City in 2017, has ever matched that feat.

A 6-5 point guard, the Big O could score or pass or rebound as well as most anyone. Oscar Robertson led his Indiana high school team to a 62-1 record and two state titles. At the University of Cincinnati, he led the country in scoring three times. At the 1960 Olympics, he was the co-captain of the gold-medal-winning United States team. The team finished 9-0 and won its games by an average of 42 points.

Robertson played in the NBA in an **era** when centers ruled the court. In his 15 pro seasons, only one non-center was ever named MVP—the Big O, in 1964. He also won an NBA title with the Milwaukee Bucks in 1971.

The Big O is the NBA's all-time leader in triple-doubles, with 181. Magic Johnson is second with 138.

NUMBERS, NUMBERS

In his amazing 1961-62 season, Robertson posted the first full-season triple-double.

Points per game: 30.8

Assists per game: 11.4

Rebounds per game: 12.5

BILL RUSSELL

In his 13 seasons with the Boston Celtics, Bill Russell won 11 NBA championships. He has more rings than fingers.

"Russ," a 6-10 **center**, has the lowest career scoring average of anyone in this book—15.1 points per game. He showed that it's not all about scoring, winning five MVP trophies.

What made Russell so valuable? He was the best defensive player of his time, and perhaps of all time. He is second all-time in rebounds and is considered the top shot-blocker in league history. Russell was a leader. He made players around him play even better. There have been greater players than Russell, but there was never a player who was better at making his team great.

In 1968, Russell was made the player-coach of the Celtics. He was the first African American to lead an NBA team.

NUMBERS, NUMBERS

Bill Russell's 11 NBA championships are tied for the most of any pro athlete in a North American sport. Here are the tops in each sport.

Player, Team	League	Titles
Bill Russell, Celtics	NBA	11
Henri Richard, Canadiens	NHL	11
Yogi Berra, Yankees	MLB	10
Tom Brady, Patriots	NFL*	5
Charles Haley, 49ers/Cowboys	NFL*	5

*Super Bowls only

WILT CHAMBERLAIN

PHILADELPHIA/SAN FRANCISCO WARRIORS
PHILADELPHIA 76ERS • LOS ANGELES LAKERS

Massive and muscular, the 7-1 Wilt Chamberlain was one of a kind. More than 40 years since he retired, the numbers "Wilt the Stilt" put up remain unchallenged.

On March 2, 1962, Chamberlain scored 100 points in a game against the New York Knicks. Seriously! The closest anyone has ever come to that record since was Kobe Bryant with 81 in a 2006 game.

You think scoring 50 points in a game is cool? Wilt *averaged* that many points per game in 1961-62. In his first five seasons, Chamberlain never averaged fewer than 36.9 points per game. Only one other NBA player has ever done that even *once*. (Michael Jordan averaged 37.1 in 1986-87.) Of the top 54 highest-scoring games in league history, Chamberlain, a four-time league MVP, has 29 of them.

Could he rebound? Chamberlain is the NBA's all-time rebounds leader. He holds the single-game record with 55.

In 14 NBA seasons, Chamberlain never fouled out of a game. That is even more incredible—he averaged more minutes per game (45:48) than anyone in league history.

No other player has ever led the NBA in both scoring and rebounding in the same season. Chamberlain did that *five times*. He holds the NBA single-season records for highest scoring average (50.4 points) and highest rebounding average (27.2). "The Big Dipper," as he was also known, even led the league in assists one year.

What Babe Ruth was to baseball, Chamberlain is to basketball: a figure who came along and shattered the ceiling of what fans and players thought was possible.

NUMBERS, NUMBERS

Top Five Single-Season NBA Scoring Marks

(Per-game average)

1. Chamberlain	50.4, 1962
2. Chamberlain	44.9, 1963
3. Chamberlain	38.4, 1961
4. Chamberlain	37.6, 1960
5. Michael Jordan	37.1, 1987

KAREEM ABDUL-JABBAR

MILWAUKEE BUCKS • LOS ANGELES LAKERS

Besides being the tallest player on our list at 7-2, Kareem Adbul-Jabbar is the most prolific. Do you know what "prolific" means? It means you get a lot of stuff done.

No one in NBA history ever played more minutes (57,446), scored more points (38,387), appeared in more All-Star Games (19), or won more Most Valuable Player awards (six) than Abdul-Jabbar. He towers over everyone on this list in more ways than one.

He was born Lew Alcindor in New York City. He led his high school team to 71 consecutive victories. Then he moved across the country and led his college team, UCLA, to three straight national championships. Because of Alcindor's skill, the NCAA (the group that oversees college sports) briefly outlawed the dunk. Can you imagine that?

Since retiring, Abdul-Jabbar has kept busy writing books. One of them is about African American sports heroes. Another is a novel that stars characters from Sherlock Holmes.

He joined the NBA's Milwaukee Bucks in 1969. He invented his own shot, the skyhook. It was unstoppable because Abdul-Jabbar released it with his body shielding the ball from the defender and the ball atop his outstretched arm. When the ball left his fingers, it was above the rim. The skyhook was a work of art.

In 1971, he changed his name after converting to Islam. Abdul-Jabbar played his first six seasons with the Milwaukee Bucks. He led them to the 1971 NBA championship. He spent his final 14 seasons with the Los Angeles Lakers, teaming up with Magic Johnson to win five NBA Finals. It almost goes unnoticed that he is third all-time in rebounds (behind two other players on our list, Wilt Chamberlain and Bill Russell) and blocked shots.

Abdul-Jabbar played with elegance and style and poured in more points than any other player.

NUMBERS, NUMBERS

Abdul-Jabbar is the NBA's all-time leader in field goals. That's NBA talk for any shot that goes in the basket, not counting free throws.

Most Field Goals

Kareem Abdul-Jabbar	15,836
Karl Malone	13,443
Wilt Chamberlain	12,681

LeBRON JAMES

CLEVELAND CAVALIERS • MIAMI HEAT

When he was a high school junior, LeBron James made the cover of *Sports Illustrated*. The magazine called him "The Chosen One." That's a lot to live up to, but "King James" has more than proven himself.

Through the 2017 season, James appeared in seven straight NBA Finals. That's the most by any player other than those on the great 1960s Celtics teams. He was the 2004 Rookie of the Year, a four-time league MVP, and a 14-time All-Star. James is big (6-8), fast, and strong. He excels both on defense and offense. Only three players have a higher career scoring average than James's 27.16 points per game.

James grew up in Akron, Ohio, and led his high school team to national titles. He decided to skip college, and it proved to be the right move.

James is the youngest player in NBA history to reach 30,000 career points. He reached that mark in 2018 at the age of 33.

He joined the Cleveland Cavaliers, making all his Ohio fans very happy. By 2007, he led the Cavaliers to the NBA Finals. However, they were swept 4-0 by the San Antonio Spurs. James wanted to bring a title to Ohio, but thought it was time to try somewhere else. In 2010, he announced that would play for the Miami Heat. He told the news in a live TV show. It was a huge deal, but made Ohio fans sad. James was criticized for "The Decision." Still, he led the Heat to four straight NBA Finals, winning two.

In 2014, he thrilled hometown fans again by returning to the Cavs. Teaming with ace guard Kyrie Irving, they dominated the East. Cleveland played in the NBA Finals from 2015 through 2017. They lost to Golden State in 2015, but got revenge in 2016. Down three games to one, the Cavs made a huge rally. Led by James, they won three straight to capture the title. It was the biggest comeback in NBA playoff history. Cleveland finally had its champion. The King had brought the crown to his hometown.

NUMBERS, NUMBERS

All-Time Postseason Scoring (Through 2017)

LeBron James	6,163
Michael Jordan	5,987
Kareem Abdul-Jabbar	5,762
Kobe Bryan	5,640
Shaquille O'Neal	5,250

MICHAEL JORDAN

CHICAGO BULLS • WASHINGTON WIZARDS

Anyone who saw Michael Jordan perform will probably say that he is the greatest basketball player ever. Certainly, no player was better under pressure.

Jordan is the league's all-time leader in points per game (30.12) and third all-time in steals per game (2.35). The 6-6 guard was a 14-time All-Star and a five-time NBA MVP. What made him so special is that no one ever played with a greater desire to win. In the 1990s, Jordan took the Chicago Bulls to six NBA Finals and the Bulls won all six. No team even took the Bulls to a Game 7. The MVP of all six of those Finals was "MJ."

A key part of Jordan's game is found in the name of the shoe Nike created for him: Air Jordan.

NUMBERS, NUMBERS

Jordan's 1995-96 Bulls finished 72-10, which at the time was the best regular-season record in NBA history. The teams that had the three top records in league history all have someone from our list:

2015-16 Warriors	73-9 (Curry)
1995-96 Bulls	72-10 (Jordan)
1971-72 Lakers	69-13 (Chamberlain)
1996-97 Bulls	69-13 (Jordan)

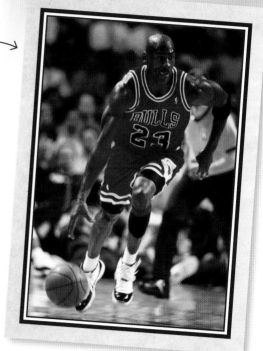

MJ is the NBA's all-time leader in points-per-game playoff scoring (33.45). He set a single-game playoff record with 63 points in 1986.

Jordan seemed to **defy** gravity as he soared to the rim. His spectacular dunks left fans and foes in awe in NBA arenas everywhere. Dunks are common today, but it was Jordan who made it cool to "play above the rim."

Another reason Jordan was so great is that when the pressure was on, he came through. As a freshman at North Carolina, he hit the game-winning shot in the 1982 national title game versus Georgetown. In 1989, he hit the buzzer-beating, series-winning shot in the Eastern Conference playoffs against the Cleveland Cavaliers.

In Game 6 of the 1998 NBA Finals, his Bulls trailed by one with 19 seconds left. Jordan stole the ball from another all-time great, Karl Malone. Then he dribbled down court and buried a championship-winning jumper. These are just three examples of Jordan's heroics, but there are too many to count.

When MJ played, he was a superhero in sneakers. No matter what team you rooted for, everyone was a Michael Jordan fan.

YOUR TOP TEN!

In this book, we listed our Top 10, but not in order of greatness. We gave you some facts and information about each player. Now it's your turn to put the players in order. Find a pen and paper. Now make your own list! Who should be the No. 1 hoopster of all time? How about your other nine choices? Would they be the same players? Would they be in the same order as they are in this book? Are any players missing from this book? Who would you include? Do you just list them in order of how many points they scored? It's your call!

Remember, there are no wrong answers. Every fan might have different choices. You should be able to back up your choices, though. If you need more information, go online and learn. Or find other books about these great hoopsters. Then discuss the choices with your friends!

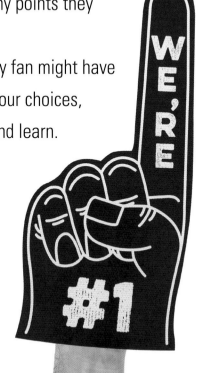

THINK ABOUT THIS . . .

Here are some things to think about when making your own Top 10 list:

- How did each player help his team win?
- How important were the shots the player hit?
- What made each player a champion?
- What players did we leave off this list?
- When did he play? Has basketball changed over time?

21

SPORTS GLOSSARY

assists (us-SISTS) passes that lead directly to a successful shot

center (SEN-ter) basketball position that usually plays near the basket

defy (dee-FY) ignore, refuse to agree

era (AIR-uh) a specific time period

power forward (POW-er FOR-wurd) a basketball position that focuses on shooting and rebounding

three-point arc (THREE POYNT ARK) the line on the court beyond which players shoot for three points

triple-double (TRIPP-el DUBB-ul) reaching double digits in three stats in one game or season

FIND OUT MORE

IN THE LIBRARY

Christopher, Matt. *Michael Jordan: Legends in Sports.* New York, NY: Little Brown Books for Young Readers, 2009.

Christopher, Matt. *On the Court with Stephen Curry.* New York, NY: Little Brown Books for Young Readers, 2017.

Wiseman, Blaine. *Basketball Legends.* Calgary, AL: Weigl Books, 2017.

ON THE WEB

Visit our Web site for links about Top 10 basketball superstars: **childsworld.com/links**

Note to Parents, Teachers, and Librarians: We routinely verify our Web links to make sure they are safe and active sites. So encourage your readers to check them out!

INDEX

Abdul-Jabbar, Kareem, 14-15
"Air Jordan," 19
Alcindor, Lew, 14
Bird, Larry, 6
Boston Celtics, 6, 11, 16
Chamberlain, Wilt, 12-13, 15
Chicago Bulls, 18, 19
Cincinnati Royals, 10
Cleveland Cavaliers, 16, 17
Curry, Stephen, 7
Duncan, Tim, 8
Golden State Warriors, 7, 17
Irving, Kyrie, 17
James, LeBron, 4, 5, 16-17
Johnson, Earvin "Magic," 9, 15

Jordan, Michael, 5, 8, 12, 18-19
Kerr, Steve, 7
Los Angeles Lakers, 9, 12, 15
Malone, Karl, 19
Miami Heat, 17
Milwaukee Bucks, 10, 14
Olympics, 10
Robertson, Oscar "The Big O," 10
Russell, Bill, 11, 15
Ruth, Babe, 13
San Antonio Spurs, 8, 17
UCLA, 14
University of North Carolina, 19
Wake Forest, 8
Westbrook, Russell, 10

ABOUT THE AUTHOR

John Walters wrote for *Sports Illustrated* and *Newsweek* and worked for NBC Sports at the Summer Olympics. He earned two Sports Emmys for his work there. He is the author of *The Same River Twice: A Season With Geno Auriemma and the Connecticut Huskies*, *Notre Dame Golden Moments*, and is a co-author of *Basketball for Dummies*.